THE MODERN YOUNG MAN'S GUIDE TO MANHOOD

The Unfiltered Version

Wayne Walker

© Copyright 2023 by Wayne Walker, All rights reserved.

This book was written with the goal of providing information that is as accurate and reliable as possible. Professionals should be consulted as needed before undertaking any of the actions endorsed herein.

This declaration is deemed fair and valid by both the American Bar Association and the Committee of Publishers Association and is legally binding throughout the United States.

Furthermore, the transmission, duplication or reproduction of any of the following work, including precise information, will be considered an illegal act, irrespective whether it is done electronically or in print. The legality extends to creating a secondary or tertiary copy of the work or a recorded copy and is only allowed with express written consent of the Publisher. All additional rights are reserved.

The information in the following pages is broadly considered to be a truthful and accurate account of facts, and as such any inattention, use or misuse of the information in question by the reader will render any resulting actions solely under their purview. There are no scenarios in which the publisher or the original author of this work can be in any fashion deemed liable for any hardship or damages that may befall them after undertaking information described herein.

TABLE OF CONTENTS

THE MOTIVATIONS 5

MY STORY 7

MEN'S ESSENTIALS 11

YOUR CAREER 15

MONEY 19

MENTAL HEALTH 27

LANGUAGES AND THE ARTS 29

TRAVEL 33

PROTECTING YOURSELF AND OTHERS 35

QUICK ANSWERS: DEALING WITH 43

WOMEN 49

THE NEED FOR GOOD MEN 57

CONCLUSION 59

TRAVEL EXTRA 61

RESOURCES 67

PROFILE OF THE AUTHOR 69

THE MOTIVATIONS

I am the father of a son! I have been able to share a lot of what I know with him, but there are certain things that would be better to have in a guide that he can refer to. It is this need that led me to write the book. My other motivation is that I wanted to create a manual for young men in general, who are making the transition into manhood.

MY STORY

Any book of this type requires a little background on the writer so that there is a better understanding for some of the opinions that are in it. This understanding can also alert the reader to any potential bias that might leak into the work.

The brief background on me is; I am the son of Caribbean immigrants and I grew up in New York City. I have been living on and off in Europe for 20+ years and my travels have taken me to 30 countries. I have lived in, not just visited, Sweden, Denmark, United States, Jamaica, Spain, and the United Kingdom.

Professionally, most of my life has been in the worlds of finance and entrepreneurship.

The family

My relationship with my father, now deceased, was strained at different times in my life, but the important thing for me was that he was there! I was able to see the qualities in him that I wanted to assimilate; ambition, honor, and masculinity, while careful to minimize the influence of other areas that I found undesirable; overly stubborn and insensitivity. My loving mother, also deceased, played an equally important role in my life, but she was not a man nor could she replace one. Not to mention, it would have been an unfair request to place on her, or any woman, to be a man, and a woman at the same time. Being a woman is enough work.

At the time of writing there are some forces that are attempting to convince us that men and women are more or less interchangeable and that there are no real differences. I must, with all due respect, state that this is absolute nonsense. Equal, yes, but the same, no. More on this in the later chapters.

MEN'S ESSENTIALS

Only you can validate you

Before we get into the more concrete topics we must begin with the most challenging part of manhood...dealing with yourself and working on your mind. The mind is where the real battle is for many things. In sports, people are quick to say the mental game is more difficult or at the very least, just as important as the physical. From personal experience with sports and competition in general, I can confirm it to be true. Obviously sports is not the only place that the mental game plays a role. It could, for example, be a job interview or going on a first date with the woman of your dreams.

The most important part of the mental game is understanding that no one can validate you and you do not need validation from anyone, no man or woman. Your worth, or value, is up to you, and what you place on it. Unfortunately, it took me many years to fully understand and assimilate this point into my way of thinking. Don't misunderstand me, I have had self confidence for most of my life and a lot of that was developed from competing in sports (wrestling, swimming, marathon running, etc.). Even with all of that confidence, I still felt at different times in my life, that things would be better, if some person or group would just accept me. When I was in university it was more about getting the affection of different girls. I only wished I had known then what I finally understood after university, the less attention paid to women the more of them you seem to have.

In a professional workplace this concept of not needing validation can be tougher to execute because you are working for someone else or a company. However, you must be alert to knowing your value and protect it. One of the best analogies I have heard that explained this concept, is about the pricing of water. Bottled water is more or less a commodity now a days. The bottled water companies can slap whatever label they want on their bottles, but we are still talking about water. A brand of bottled water can cost almost nothing at the corner store, but in the cafe at my local opera house the price is triple for the same brand. All I did was change the location of where I bought the water. The lesson to learn is, if you are in a situation where you feel that you need validation from others, you are just in the wrong place. Change your location and your value might triple.

Just get to the next step

One of the most life changing things that you can learn on your manhood journey is the idea of just getting to the next step. This concept is nothing that I invented, it is well known by soldiers completing special forces training. They know that when pushed to the breaking point mentally or physically, that the way to survive is not to think any further than the next step. For example, you have 200 push-ups to do, resist thinking about number 200. If you are at 15 then work to get to 16 and so on. I have *never* been a special forces soldier but in this area of mental strength we can all learn a lot from them.

Many times when you have a big goal, things can just seem overwhelming, almost impossible. What has helped me through some of the most difficult challenges in my life is just understanding that all I needed to do was get to the next step, and continue repeating the process. I promise you, apply this to just about anything and you will get further than you can ever imagine.

By they way, I have applied this way of thinking to write almost all the books that I have written. Almost always when I begin a book, things appear too much, but once I get going the words seem to find me instead of me searching for them. Besides writing, it helps me with business projects, and of course sports, one of the things that keep me sane.

YOUR CAREER

Speaking at an event at NASDAQ OMX

I don't want to waste your time, therefore I must get straight to the point. The most important thing that you can do to advance your career is to develop your network. This network is the connection of people you know and who they know. I am not totally crazy, clearly your education and professional experiences are important, but a good network beats all these things with ease. In my life there are several examples of this. From having a speaking event at the Royal Danish Embassy in Moscow (2019), to a live radio broadcast across Latin America, all, were in large part due to my network. Of course I needed to have something of value to deliver, but having a strong network is the "steroids" needed to accelerate the process.

When you examine the great accomplishments of just about anyone, you will see, and they will almost always reveal the importance of having a great network. I challenge you to examine your own life so far and look at the big things that have happened, positively or negatively, and see what role your network played.

Getting the network

The quickest way to get a network, is by being of service to others first. Just running around to different persons or groups trying to see what you can grab from them is not productive in the short or long term. You will be quickly blocked on all the social media platforms and avoided in real life. People are not stupid, they can sense the energy of those who are only looking to get something with no intention of giving anything in return. To be very clear, I am in no way suggesting that you should just give, give, give like a fool. What I am suggesting, is that you connect with similar minded people who embrace the idea of give and take.

You are NOT on the team!

This is one of the more painful things that I have had to write about. What I am referring to, of you not being on the team, has to do with the family feeling that many companies try to instill in their employees. They suggest that you and they are part of a team or a family. This is probably the biggest corporate lie ever told by many companies across the world. I write this knowing that no company will ever hire me again if they read this book because myself and others are exposing their big lie.

I have worked at many companies in the United States and Europe and the results are similar. They all have the "we are a team" posters, company picnics, team building events, Christmas parties, etc. but if at anytime, there is a problem with revenues and they need to lower expenses, you will be fired within minutes. Established firms or new technology startups operate equally feelings less. There are enough references on the internet that describe how groups of people were fired by online video meetings. Others do it by gathering everyone into a room where the employees are given envelopes, then they are asked to open them, and the envelopes reveal to each employee if they stay or go. This happened at one company where I worked. This was from the same company that told these people how valuable they were and that they were all a "family"…until there was a problem.

Please, for your mental and financial protection, always, always, be aware you are <u>not</u> on the team. Learn as much as you can, do the best job possible, and make good connections, but never fall into the "we are all a big family" trap, because you are not.

MONEY

I was thinking about what kind of smooth or more diplomatic title that I could use for this chapter, but in the end I decided on "Money" to skip the games and get immediately down to business. Money, in my world is really just another way of saying options. The more money you have or have access to, the more options that you possess. It is really that simple.

This is not an investing book, but I have written several about all types of asset classes and some are listed in the resources section. My goal in this chapter is to provide you with a good base of investing principles that you can build further on. I mentioned in the career chapter,"you are not on the team", therefore, to protect yourself, starting to invest and create assets outside of being employed by a company is essential for your financial security.

Stocks

You will begin with a good mix of stocks from different sectors.

Blue Chip stocks: Most investors will begin building a portfolio here. These stock are from well known and stable companies that many will know, for example IBM.

Speculative stocks: Are those with a relatively high risk rating, but they have the potential for beyond average growth, for example Tesla.

Dividend stocks: Are companies that share their profits with shareholders by giving regular payouts. Dividends can only be paid from profits, therefore it is a sign of a well managed company.

These payouts can be used as income or reinvested. I often recommend these type stocks for first time investors. Johnson & Johnson is an example of a dividend stock.

Cyclical stocks: Their results are closely tied to the cycles of the broader economy. They are trend following. An example would be Apple.

Growth stocks: The companies with the potential for faster than average growth in their sectors. Netflix could be considered a growth stock (at the time of writing).

Defensive stocks: Are considered stable and reliable regardless of market conditions. The stocks that you can sleep on, but keep in mind there are no guarantees with any stock.

Index funds

Index funds (passive) are preferred to actively managed funds. My basis for the preference is simple, over time, the majority of actively managed funds underperform the market. Index funds are created to track or mirror the composition of a market index. Some examples are the Dow Jones Industrial Average (DJIA) or the Nasdaq Composite. The average index fund historically beats the average managed funds by a few percentage points.

The clear advantage of index funds is that they have a lower expense ratio. Their cost of doing business is simply lower. Index funds make fewer trades and have smaller staffs, which results in lower expenses. This is possible because the goal of the manager is only to copy the index that the fund is tracking. The reality is that you can have actively managed funds that initially outperform an index fund, but after accounting for the expenses from trades and the more expensive management teams, they lose.

While I prefer index funds to other funds, it is important to state that they are NOT risk free. They are tracking an index therefore that index's performance, good or bad, will be reflected in the fund's performance.

Alternative investments - cryptocurrencies

Cryptocurrencies, also called cryptos, are not part of the traditional investment mix but they should be. They qualify, because as an asset class they do not normally correlate with other assets, for example, stocks or commodities. They can also serve as a hedge (offset the risk) to your other investments.

This recommendation is not about how I personally feel about them, it is simply to answer the question "will they add value to a diversified portfolio?" the answer is a clear yes. The market returns of Bitcoin, *over time*, when compared to stocks, are astonishingly in favor of Bitcoin. For those who still hold the view that this is a fad, or will just go away, the facts to date, are not in your favor.

Warning: I must mention that cryptos can be *very* volatile, if you are uncomfortable with volatility, stay away. New investors would also only want to have a small portion of their portfolios exposed to cryptos.

What should you have in your crypto portfolio?

Select a few and get to know them well. As you can imagine, it is not the norm for an investor to have exposure to 50 different cryptos in a portfolio. Most people begin crypto investing by buying the most well-known ones, for example Bitcoin and Ethereum. After a while, they begin to expand their crypto universe as they get a better understanding of how cryptos move.

Entrepreneurship

Entrepreneurship is a necessary part of every man's toolkit. I remain surprised as to why so *few* people have made a side-career or a part-time business plan, for just in case.

Begin slowly

No one needs to suddenly leave their job or turn their life upside down. Starting a business while still employed allows you to avoid the stress of the financial uncertainty that is common when you are starting. If you do end up in the great situation of having a profitable side business, then you can continue growing it until it replaces your job income. I should also state there are several potential tax advantages that go along with having a side business. The tax rules are different from country to country, I would recommend that you speak with a local tax professional.

Growing your business knowledge

The skills of running a business, unsurprisingly, are developed from deliberate practice and coaching. Taking classes can be useful, but ultimately you will need the guidance of someone who has or had a profitable business. Done correctly, this will save you time, and in the long run, money.

An Excerpt from my book, _Your First Startup: (Book 2), The Next Steps,_ which has been able to help many along the way on their journey to entrepreneurship.

Excerpt from, _Your First Startup: (Book 2), The Next Steps_

Mindset

This topic is always part of my business books because it is more critical than any technology or business strategy. If you do not have the correct mindset for running a scalable business, then all the software in the world will be useless to you.

Well, the obvious question is what is this "mindset" thing? Is it just more fake motivation, make you feel good nonsense of so-called gurus? Not at all, it is simply having the discipline to continue the journey no matter what happens. Many people develop this "continue moving ahead no matter what" mental strength from sports (I did). Luckily, it is not the only way to develop this type of strength, one example I love to use is classical musicians. Anyone that has met one knows of the hours they spend perfecting their craft. Many of the people who overcome the rough times that will come from business usually have some other area that helped them develop this trait. Remember, that even the smallest steps still move you forward.

Success

A key part of mindset is determining for yourself what success is for you. Avoid the trap of copying other people's views of success. For you, it might be income to supplement what you earn at your job or it could be to replace the job altogether. Another person might have a goal that is more philanthropic, for example, making a change in society that has nothing to do with making a financial profit. Please keep in mind that a non-profit organization is not the same as for-loss. Even these organizations need and use many principles of the startup world.

Once you have determined what success is for you, then the steps needed to accomplish it must be taken. It has been told to me many times and it remains true: "We do not step into or just arrive into the future; we create it from what we are doing today." What you harvest in six months or six years, fairly or unfairly, is mostly from what you are planting now. I suggest that you ask yourself, "What am I planting?"

You might have noticed that I left out real estate from the money section. This is because as an asset class, the initial capital requirements are much larger. You can begin investing in stocks with $100, but this amount is normally not realistic for real estate.

MENTAL HEALTH

Mental health is finally being treated with the same seriousness as physical health, and I am very happy about that. While this is not a mental health guide, I do want to express that you as a man can experience or feel all different types of things mentally and it is okay to get help from professionals.

In the past this was a no touch topic because of the old fashion opinions that masculine men didn't have feelings. Gladly, this antique way of thinking is being phased out and replaced by reality and the obvious truth; men have feelings. Whether it is anxiety, excessive stress, depression, you name it, us men might experience these conditions at some point in our lives.

The outdated image of a man suffering alone on a mountain top is unhealthy for anyone, and it has been the cause of so many problems for us guys in the past. Being masculine also means being aware of your mental state. During the periods of my life where there have been unhealthy amounts of stress, speaking with a professional, or a few close friends really helped me a lot. I am also a fan of meditating, but again, I stress these are things that worked for my specific situations and each person is different.

LANGUAGES AND THE ARTS

Languages

A must do, any man that is still monolingual, in our super connected world, is like fighting with only one hand when he could have two or more. Learning a second or a third language is another of those activities that has no downsides. It is a plus for business, career, or pleasure, and especially pleasure in my case.

My native language is English, but I speak 3 other languages more or less fluently. The others are Spanish, Danish, and Caribbean Creole (patois). For me, learning languages has opened up several business opportunities, for example, giving a live broadcast across Latin America about cryptocurrencies. The network of friends that I have has expanded dramatically over the years because of my language skills. I am sure you will experience something similar if you take the steps of learning another language.

Best language?

There is no best language, I would suggest that you begin with the one that grabs your interest. Outside of a personal interest, then you will probably want to focus on the ones with a large base of native speakers. This makes it easier to find partners to practice with. For the curious, my next languages to learn are Portuguese and Italian. They make sense for me since I already speak Spanish.

Develop an appreciation of the arts

The fine arts are what many people gradually assimilate into their lives. First, we define the arts that I am referring to: opera, modern dance, ballet, and theater. I will also add museums, while they are not art, you will find many types of art in them.

What you will experience by increasing your exposure to the arts is a deeper understanding of yourself in an intimate way. Whether it is a famous painting or seeing a dance performance, unless you are dead, it will move you emotionally. I remember seeing the Alvin Alley Dance Company at Tivoli Gardens in Copenhagen, Denmark and it took days for the experience to leave me.

My path to appreciation of the arts started early, and it has played a greater role in my life as time goes on. I was luckily enough to attend a high school that made the fine arts an important part of the curriculum. Therefore I was exposed to great museums, etc. for many years.

In university, the love of the arts slowed down because I was too busy with traveling and chasing girls. However, there was one magic period of time. I had a part-time job at the Museum of Modern Art (MoMA) in New York City, which was one of the defining moments in my life. The experience for me was similar to attending an art appreciation academy, that paid you to learn. My appreciation and love of the arts exploded!

I am aware not everyone is able to get a summer job at MoMA, but you don't need to, just begin visiting the museums located where you live. What you might notice is that one art leads you to another. In my case it was the amazing works of art (paintings) that led me to opera. I took it even further because I started working with and performing at the Royal Danish Opera, not as a singer, but as a Supporting Character (an Extra) in different productions.

Where you begin your journey into the arts is not overly critical, you just need to begin and see how much you will learn about yourself.

TRAVEL

Get away from home! You might have heard of foreign travel being recommended before by others and I am here to agree with them. Traveling as much as your wallet will allow you, is an activity that gives you benefits long after the trips are over. Even a bad trip has lessons that you will learn from. My experiences with travel began as a child when my family moved to the United States and I have never stopped.

One of the most important benefits of foreign travel is that it gives you an opportunity to challenge a lot of the things you know about life and other cultures. Your biases and prejudices will get a little test. I grew up in the American system with a Caribbean twist, but basically I am a New Yorker who also spent a lot time in Southern California. This sums up my starting point of how I viewed a lot of the world before I started to travel more internationally.

The bottom line with traveling abroad is, that you will discover, if you are open minded, that the way you and your country interprets and does things might not be the best. The ideal result will be, that after a few travels abroad, you will not be so quick to judge other cultures that are different from yours.

PROTECTING YOURSELF AND OTHERS

Being a man also means having the ability to defend yourself and others that you care about. I would also extend the definition to protecting the innocent but maybe that is just me and not everyone wants to go that far.

Violence

Men should have a certain level of understanding of violence, because as a man, statistically, you are more likely to experience it than a woman.* This phenomenon is often referred to as the "fear of crime gender paradox". As a reader of this book, you are most likely a part of the majority of men who are not violent as a norm. I also consider myself a member of this club, in the sense that I *do not* advocate random violence. However, I am aware that not everyone believes in this and you should be too. This means you must be prepared to defend yourself and bring pain to those that will harm you or those that you care about.

*https://www.sbs.com.au/news/the-feed/article/myth-busting-the-true-picture-of-gendered-violence/hbbqupyt8

*https://en.wikipedia.org/wiki/Violence_against_men

Where to get this understanding

Martial arts and full contact sparring are two of the best ways to get some level of comfort with rough physical contact in a relatively safe environment.

In this brief section I will share my opinions on what I found to be the most useful self-defense art form. I am not a professional fighter, nor will I ever claim to be one, because I am not. After meeting a few and having trained with them I certainly have nothing but respect for anyone willing to enter the rings of professional combat sports.

Filipino martial arts (FMA)

I would suggest that you learn one of the Filipino martial arts, for example, Escrima. I have trained it for many years, and in the few situations where I had to defend myself physically, it was very useful. Knowing it gives me a certain self confidence that is difficult to put into words, so I will just write that it is a good feeling.

Why FMA?

Why these martial arts and not others?, because they are often weapons based, but the most important are the mental aspects of them. You will learn to see almost everything as a potential tool that can be used to protect yourself, which is comforting. It becomes almost a game after a while. Every time I enter a new environment, I automatically scan the room for what I can use to protect myself.

The training of Escrima begins with one or two wooden or rattan sticks. From the outside it might look a little strange. It appears that people are just hitting with sticks, in reality the sticks are just an extension of their arms. Or explained another way, the movements that you make with the sticks, if you dropped them (the sticks), the empty hand movements, would be the same. This is the beauty of Escrima, you learn two things at the same time, to defend yourself armed and unarmed with the same movements.

Being in one of the popular environments of men, especially young men, meaning bars, there are bottles, bar stools, chairs, etc. that might be used against you. Knowing one of the Filipino martial arts gives you an advantage because you will practice, defending against, and using all these items and more (in self-defense), during your classes. FMA's are *not* the perfect martial arts, but they are a good start.

Outside of the Filipino martial arts, I would also suggest training one of the grappling sports. They can be useful for controlling people without permanently hurting them. I had the luck of wrestling competitively for many years, beginning in high school. This experience gave me a lot of practice with grappling and body control. There are other sports that can also teach you similar techniques, for example Judo.

Things to consider

Whenever people learn self-defense, I also recommend that they become familiar with the legal realities. This is not the cool part, but, everyone should know the self-defense laws in their country. The laws can vary dramatically from country to country, and if you are in the United States, from state to state.

Most places do have the principle that you can only use force that is proportional to the situation or threat. For example, if someone slaps you, you can *not* shoot them. Another principle is, just because someone insults you verbally, or says something that you don't like, you can't physically attack them. Finally, if you do become highly trained in any martial art, the courts will usually hold you to a higher standard of responsibility.

Firearms

This is not for everyone, but I would also suggest that you get some firearms training. Having a basic familiarity with firearms is not the same as saying that you need to go out and buy a hundred guns and become a fanatic living in a cave. I had the good fortune of completing a tactical shooting course in Poland where I learned to shoot on the move, and shooting while protecting others. It was a great experience! I do not own a firearm and I have *no* plans to buy one, but I do believe it is good to know how to use one safely should the need ever arise.

Saving others

Being a resource to your family and friends also means knowing how to react to health emergencies. Taking some type of first aid course is really recommended. I would suggest a course that goes deeper than just the basic CPR, and has a special focus on trauma (broken bones, burns, etc). When I was in Poland, I also completed an intensive first aid trauma course, and it really helped me to understand how quickly things can go very wrong if certain injuries are not treated immediately.

Having the confidence that I would know what to do if someone near me is injured and has some form of medical emergency is a great feeling. This feeling is something that I would like more people to have. The great news for those who are considering taking a course is that once you understand the basic principles you can begin applying them to different emergency situations.

The basics:

- Either you or someone call for an ambulance, and begin by giving your location. You would be surprised at how many forget this.

- Check if the person is breathing (the emergency phone operators will also want to know this)

- Clear the breathing pathways: making sure that nothing is blocking the throat

- Search for any signs of bleeding. If found, apply direct pressure to stop it

Obviously, these tips do not replace taking a course but they are a little preview of what any good course will focus on with hands-on practice of different scenarios.

Getting and staying fit

Staying fit is a relatively cheap life insurance policy. It seems like every other month there is some new scientific report finding yet another benefit of keeping your body fit.

I would encourage doing something that gets your body in motion. There is no need to spend excessive hours in the gym or training every day to reap the benefits of exercise. Ideally you are training 3 to 4 times a week, but you can stay reasonably fit by doing less. You will not make any Olympic team, but that is not the goal of most people, and it is probably not yours either.

If you don't want to go to a gym then find some sport that you like and begin. In this book I have made several references to sports because they have been and continue to play an important role in my life.

Injury avoidance

Going to the gym is great, but I become really upset when I get injured and it prevents me from keeping my training routine.

What is injury avoidance? It is listening to the signals that you get from your body. When you feel pains beyond the normal, it is a sign to lower the weight amount that you lift or do less repetitions of whatever you are doing. Forget the macho nonsense of doing things until you break. Challenging yourself and pushing your body is always good, but when you are in serious pain, take a break. Every time I stupidly tried to train through a major pain I ended up regretting it. The last time I did something dumb like that, I was unable to train for almost two months! As I get older, I focus more on injury avoidance. No need for you to wait until you get older, start now to begin working on injury avoidance. Your body will thank you.

The extra benefits

Besides the obvious health benefits, staying fit gives you the ability to better deal with some of life's mentally stressful moments. Writing of my experience with several difficult periods in life that I have endured, I know the medicine of exercise has helped me a lot. I do not wish you difficult times, but unfortunately they do come, no one escapes, and being physically fit is a great weapon to have to help protect yourself.

Participating in a tactical shooting course

QUICK ANSWERS: DEALING WITH...

Difficult people

Difficult people are a challenge for everyone. What I have always found funny about them is that they never believe that they are difficult. Your solution? Focus on yourself and what you need to do. If you are in a group at work or on a team in sports just keep the goal the focus. Difficult people are a part of life and I am not aware of how you can be free from ever encountering them. Remember also that any "attitudes" that they might have towards you, in many cases, have very little to do with you, but more about what is going on in that person's life.

Friends

Friends should be those people that you feel this vibe or sensation of where things are just cool. You do things for them, they do things for you. There is the feeling that things are mostly in balance without anyone ever needing to count.

Your time is a precious resource, some would argue it is your most precious, therefore, those you consider as friends should be worthy of your time. Many have said, including myself, that your circle of friends is a big factor in many of the things that happen in your life.

The one unbreakable friend rule: Any friend that attempted to harm your mental health, your reputation, or your finances, never allow them back into your world. They will only return more dangerous than before.

Relatives

This is always a sensitive topic, because it is people with whom you have a blood relationship, without being asked if you wanted it. The simplest strategy for dealing with relatives is to treat them, for the most part, as you would any other friend. If they are a threat to your mental peace, or financial well being, then you must minimize your contact with them. Being a family member does not give anyone extra privileges to hurt you. From personal experience and the experience of many others, some relatives believe that they almost have a right to take advantage of others simply because they are relatives. You can't pour from an empty glass, don't let them drain you.

Enemies

Be very careful about who falls into this category. Having a different opinion does not create an enemy. Another point to be conscious about, is creating unnecessary enemies. This is because once you have created one, given the opportunity, they or their friends, will have no problems with seeing you fail. Realistically, you can't be friends with everyone, but avoid having too many people that you consider or who consider you as an enemy.

Alcohol

Enjoy it, but in my opinion, the less you touch alcohol, the easier your life will be. I am not against light casual drinking, otherwise, I would be a hypocrite since I do have a drink at certain social events or a glass of wine with some meals.

I drank, at times, too much, especially when I was attending university. After university, thankfully, the excesses decreased but there were still occasions with way too much drinking. As time went on there were some sad incidents that made me examine more closely this relationship with alcohol. There were just too many events that I ended up apologizing for after moments of excessive drinking. It took me a while to finally understand the idea that when you are out partying, you can have just as much fun by *not* drinking. Now, I drink socially, but never to excess anymore.

I am a new fan of non-alcoholic beer. Before you begin laughing, I know that non-alcoholic beers, a few years ago, tasted so badly that being able to drink one was almost a sign of bravery. That was back then, now they are so good that you might want two.

This is my story, it is not everyone's. Maybe your experience with excessive drinking was less harmful. One thing I can say for certain, I am unaware of any social movement of people complaining because they did not get to drink to excess.

Different political views

My views have been at different points on the political spectrum depending on my age and what was going on in my life.

Currently, it seems that people are just settling into groups where they pretty much only interact with other people that share similar opinions. Even worse, they view people with a different point of view as the enemy, how sad. Someone having a different political opinion from the one I have is *not* my enemy deserving harm.

I grew up in the United States and have spent the past two decades living in Europe, plus traveling across other regions, and I notice the trend of where people see persons holding different political views as the enemy. This is often the opinion of political extremists from <u>all</u> sides.

My own political views are often difficult to put in a box, because it *depends* on the issue. I must be allowed to think and examine the situation or topic to determine what is the best way to deal with it. I would consider myself politically independent, in the sense that, in theory, I could support whomever or whatever group that has the best solution for the issues that are important to me. I do *not* blindly follow any person or political party.

I am also a big fan of personal freedom. For example, I do not smoke, but that is a decision that I made for myself. I do not lecture or debate people who want to smoke, that is their personal choice.

Humans first

Even with my political views, I have close friends who are very different, but we get along. Different political views, yes, but we see each other as humans first. A concrete example that I remember clearly was during the Corona crisis, I got vaccinated, my friend did not, and he thought it was crazy that I did. He was at my place, we had dinner and talked about it, he explained his reasons, but there was no hatred, no name calling, no idiotic threats. Dinner ended, we agreed to disagree, gave each other a handshake, hug, and all went their way happy. We still train together at the gym and life goes on.

I end with, wherever you find yourself on the political chart, be cautious of any group that does not allow for differences of opinions.

WOMEN

I saved this topic for close to the end, and it was not by chance. Before men go about seeking relationships with women they need a good relationship with themselves first. You need to be in balance as much a possible with yourself before dealing with women. Being in balance does not mean perfect. Who in the world is perfect? I am not and you are probably not either.

I have dated enough women to feel confident in the validity of what you are about to read.

I am known for writing whatever I think, this can be a good or bad thing.

Women to meet

Guys, you want a woman that is always on your side, but who is also honest enough to share the truth with you. By the way, it is expected that you provide the same to the woman in your life. Ideally your main woman is someone that you are in love with, but with age I question this more and more. Being a guy can be demanding, and your goal is to acquire a romantic partner or "asset" that contributes to your mission. Hopefully, it should not be a surprise to you that women are also seeking the same for themselves.

Women to avoid

The first type to avoid are women who are confused. These confused women are those that want to play the role of a man in your relationship. For some crazy reason there is a noticeable number of women that want to play the masculine role. This is something that you can not allow and must stop immediately. The current madness of some people suggesting that men and women are the same is a partial contributor to this nonsense.

Common sense warning

I must be very clear with this topic. Masculinity should not be confused with a sense of superiority to women. My point, again, is stressing that we are different. Obviously, I also do NOT suggest being abusive to any woman. I started the book by stating that my son was a big motivation for my writing, but I also have a daughter. Any man dating her, I would expect him to treat her like a lady. I am not a fan of, or an advocate for cavemanish male attitudes. However, I am equally opposed to the current trend that is against responsible masculine behavior, no apologies.

Masculine behavior

Masculinity means being a resource to your family and others that you care about. You are clear about what you will and what you will not accept in your life. I do not mean playing the stereotypical dumb tough guy who just goes around causing trouble or being abusive. Hurting innocent people is *not* masculine, doing so would just make you the bully that everyone should avoid. In addition, being able to express your disagreements verbally without being vulgar to people is very masculine. If this is an issue for you, then study to expand your vocabulary so that you have more words in your verbal toolbox. This strengthened vocabulary will help you avoid the lazy route of just resorting to personal insults for any disagreement. We all know that the minute you begin attacking your opponent personally, and stop discussing the *topic*, you have already lost mentally.

We continue

Yes, if needed, as you read earlier, you are expected to defend or at least attempt to defend yourself and those you care for. Even for those women who claim men and women are the same, don't be fooled by them. An easy example: Imagine, you are at home asleep with your lady, it is late at night, suddenly there is a weird sound of an unknown voice in the living room, who do you believe will be expected to go out first and investigate? I say no more.

Some men are also partially responsible for the role confusion. These men are not stepping up and playing the role that they should in a relationship. Most women want a man with masculine qualities. They know that when they feel safe, mentally and physically in a relationship, their femininity will blossom. As the cliché goes this is a "win win". The guy is being himself and the woman is being her natural self.

Your goal is to be the gentleman where you express yourself and use all of your strengths constructively.

Listen to the signals!

Your ability to change people is limited, this is a truth that you must accept.

- She tells you that she has goals different from you, believe her
- She never wants children, don't waste your time trying to convince her otherwise
- She is unhappy with how things are going in your relationship, listen, and make an honest assessment of what basis there is for it
- She thinks about her ex-boyfriend more than normal...what more signals do you need? Leave!

Nice guys lose

For those unaware, being the overly nice guy is the kiss of death with women. I wrote earlier, you not being masculine forces the woman to play both roles (masculine and feminine) which is unfair to her and it is exhausting. If you have a tendency to always go along with whatever she says and you give the impression that there are no boundaries, stop it! If she has no idea of what you stand for, then things will get ugly for you. She will leave you as soon as she can, and depending on the woman, she might just take as much a possible from you before leaving.

Dealing with a breakup

If she is the one that wants to leave, let her go! Begging any woman, that wants to leave you, to stay, rarely ends well. Keep in mind that when a woman tells you that she wants to leave, she was already thinking about it for a long time (unless she caught you cheating or something crazy like that). Your begging words will have little or no effect on her and if she does stay, all power will be transferred to her. She is now the one that gets to decide from day to day if you are together as a couple, what a nightmare, plus she has lost respect for you.

It is really true what you hear from people that there is always another one (woman). I do not write this from some know-it-all status, it is because I once had my heart broken by a woman whom I believed had everything that I wanted in life. To my surprise, less than a year later I found someone *so* much better. My story, by the way, is not unique, just ask any honest guy over 30.

When the breakup is coming from your side, do not be a jerk. Be firm, but show the compassion that you would like shown to you, as always, being a man or masculine does not equal being a cruel heartbreaker. Just imagine if it were your sister, aunt, good female friend; you would want them treated humanely when a relationship ends. We all know the social world is getting smaller and smaller by the day, and you never know where you might run into this woman or her friends again. My experiences with ex-girlfriends are mostly good, I am still connected with many of them as friends and in some cases business partners.

Where are the best women from?

There is no best country. I have dated women from one end of the planet to the other. This was not something that I planned, but I have lived on a few continents and have traveled to at least 30 countries. These travels gave me a lot of opportunities to meet people and I am a friendly person.

There are several guides and videos that rate women by countries. Do not bother with them, you will only waste your time and money. First of all, you will always find exceptions to every stereotype. For example, some say women in Scandinavia (Northern Europe) are cold and without the warm emotions like women from Southern Europe, the Caribbean, Asia, Latin America, or places closer to the equator. I have lived many years in Northern Europe and there is some truth to it, from my experience. However, I can quickly think of two ex-girlfriends, Scandinavians, who would do anything for me if I needed it.

Overall, for me, it appears women from the South or closer to the equator seem to assimilate easier into my lifestyle, but that is for me. If I were Swedish, maybe I would say something completely different. My final advice in this area, is simply that you will need to date around and see who fits best with your personality.

THE NEED FOR GOOD MEN

Not having a good father or father figure in the life of a boy or a young man is one of the threats to societies across the globe. This missing father is the root of many societal problems. More often than not, young men involved in crime, having low educational achievements, or a negative self image, etc., can be often traced back to a missing *positive* father figure in their lives.* People, regardless of their political beliefs should agree on this.

If you do a quick search on the internet and you will find article after article questioning the need of men in modern society. This has been a trend, especially in Northern Europe and the certain parts of the United States. Some say this is due to the fact that women are, for much of the developed world, financially independent, and do not need men for economic survival (a good thing). The other factor, it is more or less socially acceptable for a single woman to have a child on her own in many parts of the world. Even with these two developments, I would still strongly argue, as you have read throughout the book, the role of responsible men is more important than ever.

Further reading on the need for good men:

*article UK:

https://www.theguardian.com/society/2001/apr/05/crime.penal

* article US:

https://marripedia.org/effects_of_fatherless_families_on_crime_rates

CONCLUSION

This book has been my most personal to date. Hopefully you found some new tools to tackle the challenges of manhood along with different ways of seeing things.

TRAVEL EXTRA

This section is a random collection of notes from several of my travels. These insights are clearly very subjective, just my opinions. Your experience in these countries might better or worse. Happy travels!

First trips

My first trips were across the United States border to Niagara Falls, Canada because I attended university close to the Buffalo, New York and the Niagara Falls border. The experience was not all that much different from the US and there was little to no culture shock outside of the different pronunciation of a few words.

In the middle of my university years I spent a lot of time in Mexico which was an eye opener. This was during the period when I left my university in New York to attend one located in San Diego, California, another border city. This time, Mexico was at the border. I could not believe that a city, Tijuana, which was just 15 minutes away from me could be so different, I was really naïve but I learned a lot. First, the obvious, Tijuana is not all of Mexico. This is a huge country with a strong and rich culture. I had the pleasure of going farther south in Mexico and that was a very different experience culturally.

Other travels in South America, for example Brazil, showed me the many connections that exist between some South American and Caribbean cultures.

Later travels

Europe

Traveling through Europe, so far, has been great. The trips that really stood out to me where those to Poland and Russia. I knew very little of both countries and much of what I learned in school, growing up, was not always accurate. The politics I will not touch, I am not a politician. I can only write of the people that I met and what I saw. In Russia, I spent most of my time in an embassy, so there is not much to write. When I was not in the embassy, I stayed in a luxury hotel eating caviar.

In Poland, I was living and training with military people. I had a great time, plus I also had a chance to visit some of the smaller towns. Even with the language problems (I do not speak Polish) my memory of the interactions were pleasant.

Besides these two trips, my other trips have been mostly in Western Europe, with Madrid, Lisbon, and Rome being my favorite cities.

Asia

If you get the opportunity to visit Asia I would recommend beginning with the Philippines. Filipinos are some of the kindest and friendliest people that I have ever met. Besides the amazing people you will experience great food and affordable living.

China

Since you are already in the region, China is also a stop to consider. My time there was another moment of where my views of the world were really challenged. My views were challenged so much that I am considering writing a book just on my visit to China. I was working in the cities of Nanjing and Shanghai, and again I was faced with tough questions of what I believed to be the "best" way to live. I realized that my ideal way to live, unsurprisingly, was mostly based on what was best for people who share a similar background to mine (heavily Western), but it may not be for everyone else.

The Caribbean

I also spent some time in the Caribbean. I worked a lot in Trinidad and Tobago. A country that is on my list of must revisit. A place of smiles, beaches, and a relatively good economy.

Puerto Rico

Puerto Rico from what I remember was nice. Honestly, I did not see much, I was there with some girl I met in a bar in New York city. We were stuck at a luxury hotel and a private beach.

Being a big salsa music fan, Puerto Rico is a place close to my heart. I grew up and worked in New York City, therefore, it should not be unusual that I had Puerto Rican friends. The latest news that I have from the island is that the capital, San Juan, is being invaded by crypto millionaires.

US Virgin Islands

The US Virgin Islands, St Thomas and St. Johns, just go! But you will need some money. This is not a place for budget backpack travellers. I rented a villa and it was worth the money I spent, and my girlfriend at the time agreed.

Jamaica

Jamaica is the island country that could be even more amazing if it were managed better. Many Jamaicans will say Jamaica is not poor, but poorly managed. I agree, this is a country with incredible natural wonders, beaches, culture, etc., but the real strength is the ambition of the people. Those that emigrate, for the most part, excel when they get elsewhere with better opportunities. When more of the inefficiencies in the governmental departments are corrected, then sky's the limit for my home in the sun.

RESOURCES

When You Are Ready To Continue The Manhood Journey – Contact Me

I sincerely hope that this practical book was of benefit to you. However, I also realize that books do have limitations and those that would like more hands-on coaching please contact me here: www.gcmsonline.info, where I can respond to you.

If you have not read any of my other books, then I invite you to do so, because they have valuable lessons that will be helpful to you.

Other books:

Your First Startup

Asset Class Mastery

The Next Level of Cryptocurrency Investing

The New Investing Matrix

PROFILE OF THE AUTHOR

Wayne Walker is the Director of a global capital markets education and consulting firm. He has several years experience in leading and coaching teams of Investment Advisors and has managed top performing teams in the Private Client Group based on Bench Mark Earnings (BME). Wayne has trained traders of the Citi-FX Pro program in London. He also developed the 'Trading Rights' program at a European bank by which Investment Advisors were required to complete before being allowed to trade. He is a certified trader by Markets in Financial Instrument Directive (MiFID) EU and is qualified to advise "A" clients.

Wayne is a frequently invited guest capital markets commentator on several international TV & radio programs.

Wayne holds several certifications and has worked in the following positions:

- Director-Founder, (GCMS) Global Capital Market Solutions

- Author of *Reality Based Trading Guide,(used in our classes at Copenhagen Business School & other universities in EU)*

- Manager, Sales Trading, North America & Middle East

- B.sc State University of New York, College at Buffalo, USA

- NASD Series 3 - License to trade & advise on futures contracts in the US Market

- ACI(Financial Markets) Dealing Certificate – Passed with Distinction (highest level), France

- Trained in Bloomberg & UBS Bank's FX Options quoting software

Made in the USA
Las Vegas, NV
03 March 2025